GETTING TO KNOW
THE U.S. PRESIDENTS

JIMMY
CARTER

THIRTY-NINTH PRESIDENT
1977 – 1981

WRITTEN AND ILLUSTRATED BY MIKE VENEZIA

Union Public Library

CHILDREN'S PRESS
AN IMPRINT OF SCHOLASTIC INC.
NEW YORK   TORONTO   LONDON   AUCKLAND   SYDNEY
MEXICO CITY   NEW DELHI   HONG KONG
DANBURY, CONNECTICUT

Reading Consultant: Nanci R. Vargus, Ed.D., Assistant Professor, School of Education, University of Indianapolis

Historical Consultant: Marc J. Selverstone, Ph.D., Assistant Professor, Miller Center of Public Affairs, University of Virginia

Photographs © 2008: AP Images: 17, 31; Corbis Images: 25 (Ainsworth), 7, 24, 28 (Bettmann), 27 (Maps.com), 23 (David Muench), 32 (Mark Peterson), 10 (UPI); Getty Images: 6 bottom (Hulton Archive), 30 (Karl Schumacher), 14 (George Strock), 6 top (Donald Uhrbrock); Jimmy Carter Library: 8 (National Archive), 3, 15, 19; Magnum Photos/Elliott Erwitt: 11.

Colorist for illustrations: Andrew Day

Library of Congress Cataloging-in-Publication Data

Venezia, Mike.
    Jimmy Carter / written and illustrated by Mike Venezia.
        p. cm. — (Getting to know the U.S. presidents)
    ISBN-13: 978-0-516-22643-9 (lib. bdg.)   978-0-516-25971-0 (pbk.)
    ISBN-10: 0-516-22643-6 (lib. bdg.)   0-516-25971-7 (pbk.)
    1. Carter, Jimmy, 1924—Juvenile literature 2. Presidents—United
States—Biography—Juvenile literature. I. Title.
    E873.V46 2008
    973.926092—dc22

    [B]
                                                2006102928

No part of this publication may be reproduced in whole or in part, or stored in a retrieval system, or transmitted in any form or by any means, electronic, mechanical, photocopying, recording, or otherwise, without written permission of the publisher. For information regarding permission, write to Scholastic Inc., 557 Broadway, New York, NY 10012.

© 2008 Mike Venezia.

All rights reserved. Published in 2008 by Children's Press, an imprint of Scholastic Inc. Published simultaneously in Canada. Printed in the United States of America.

SCHOLASTIC, CHILDREN'S PRESS, and associated logos are trademarks and/or registered trademarks of Scholastic Inc.

1 2 3 4 5 6 7 8 9 10 R 17 16 15 14 13 12 11 10 09 08

President Jimmy Carter at work in the Oval Office of the White House

James Earl Carter, who always preferred to be called Jimmy, was the thirty-ninth president of the United States. He was born in Plains, Georgia, on October 1, 1924. Jimmy Carter owned and ran a large peanut farm in Plains. When he decided to run for president, hardly anyone had ever heard of him!

Jimmy Carter did have some political experience. He had been a state senator and governor of Georgia. But most people outside the state weren't paying much attention to what was going on in Georgia.

Being unknown around the country didn't bother Jimmy. It just made him work harder than ever.

Jimmy believed he would make a great president and was determined to meet as many people as possible. During the presidential campaign, he traveled all over, talking to people and giving speeches day and night. When he couldn't make it to an event, he would send his wife, Rosalynn; his mom, Lillian; his son, Chip; or any other close supporter he could find to speak for him.

President Lyndon B. Johnson, shown here at his ranch in Texas, was president during the war in Vietnam.

When Jimmy Carter ran for president in 1976, everyone was pretty fed up with the government. The United States had recently been through a horrible war in Vietnam. Many people felt that Lyndon Johnson, the president during much of that time, hadn't been truthful about why the war was going on so long, or why it was even necessary. People then saw the next president, Richard Nixon, resign from office.

President Richard M. Nixon announces his resignation on August 8, 1974.

In 1976, Jimmy Carter defeated President Gerald Ford (right) to become president.

Nixon did this to avoid being fired from his job for illegal activities he was involved in. Even though Jimmy's opponent, President Gerald Ford, was an upstanding, honest man, he had been connected to the past presidents.

Jimmy Carter said that as president, he would be a newcomer to Washington, D.C., and that he'd be more open with people. Above all, he promised he would never lie to his fellow Americans. His promise was just what people wanted to hear.

A peanut farm in the South in the early 1900s

  While growing up on his family's farm,
Jimmy and his younger brother and sisters had
lots of chores to do. The Carters grew peanuts,
watermelons, sugarcane, and cotton. Jimmy's
least-favorite job was applying a mixture of
arsenic, molasses, and water to cotton buds.

This was done to prevent insects from ruining the plants. The poisonous, gooey mixture would coat Jimmy's pants and attract thousands of flies. By the end of the day, the sticky mess dried so hard that Jimmy could stand his pants up in the corner of his room.

Jimmy Carter as a young boy on his family farm near Plains, Georgia

Jimmy learned to accept most jobs he was given and usually didn't complain at all. As a young boy, Jimmy began to form lifelong feelings about religion. The Carters belonged to the Baptist Church. It was a very important part of their lives.

Early on, Jimmy formed opinions about segregation and racial injustice, too. In Georgia and other southern states, segregation was the law. It meant blacks were separated from whites. African Americans had to use their own facilities, or sections, when it came to restaurants, washrooms, drinking fountains, movie theaters, and buses.

A man drinks from a segregated water fountain in the South in 1950.

Jimmy Carter always hated the idea of segregation. Most of his neighbors were African Americans. As a young boy, Jimmy's friends were the kids of the workers on his family's farm. Jimmy felt a closeness to them and the land surrounding Plains, Georgia.

At times, though, he did dream of what it might be like to live in distant foreign lands. Jimmy read lots of adventure books. His favorite uncle, Tom Gordy, was in the navy. He often sent Jimmy postcards and letters from exciting, faraway places.

Cadets at Annapolis in the early 1940s

Jimmy always thought about joining the navy. When he graduated from high school, his parents agreed it would be a good idea for their son to attend the U.S. Naval Academy in Annapolis, Maryland. Jimmy was accepted to the academy in 1943, where he trained to be a naval officer. The United States needed lots of officers at this time to help lead soldiers during World War II.

Jimmy did really well at Annapolis. Once, on a trip back home on leave, he had a date with a friend of his sister. Her name was Rosalynn Smith. After their first date, Jimmy told his mother that Rosalynn was the girl he wanted to marry! A couple of years later, in 1946, Jimmy and Rosalynn did get married.

Jimmy and Rosalynn Carter on their wedding day, July 7, 1946

By 1946, World War II had ended. Jimmy spent the next few years in the navy testing new radar systems and training to be a submarine officer. Jimmy was even accepted into the first nuclear submarine program. This was a great honor.

As a senior officer, Jimmy studied nuclear reactor engines and trained men about the new technology. Jimmy and Rosalynn enjoyed their life in the navy. They began to raise a family and got to see different parts of the world.

Jimmy Carter was in charge of the crew that helped build the *Seawolf*, one of the first nuclear-powered submarines. This photograph shows the 1954 launching of the first nuclear-powered submarine, the USS *Nautilus*.

Then, sadly, Jimmy's father died. When Jimmy returned home for the funeral, he realized how hard his father had worked on the peanut farm. Jimmy decided then to leave the navy and return to Plains to keep the family farm running. Jimmy went back to school to learn as much as he could about farming.

After his father died, Jimmy Carter returned to Plains and expanded his family's peanut business.

He took classes in agriculture and experimented to develop new and better peanut seeds. Soon the Carter farm became very successful. Jimmy felt comfortable enough to start getting involved in his community and state government. He became a member of the school board, then ran for and was elected a state senator. In 1970, Jimmy won the election for governor of his state.

Jimmy always believed he could do some good for the citizens of Georgia. He had seen lots of things going on that bothered him very much, especially when it came to racial discrimination. While Jimmy was a state senator, he discovered that state officials were trying to prevent blacks from voting.

African Americans were forced to answer a
series of difficult questions correctly before
they were allowed to vote. Jimmy worked to
stop these and other voting-rights violations.
As governor, he continued working to end
discrimination in schools, courtrooms, and jobs.

Jimmy Carter did everything he could to simplify Georgia's government, too. He cut three hundred money-wasting departments down to twenty-five well-run departments.

As governor of Georgia, Jimmy Carter had a strong record on protecting the environment.

Jimmy always respected and loved nature. He worked hard to protect the environment of his state.

Jimmy Carter was doing a pretty remarkable job as governor. It didn't take long before he decided he might be able to do a good job as president of the United States.

A Carter supporter at the Democratic National Convention in 1976

In 1974, Jimmy announced he would run for president. Jimmy Carter's biggest problem was how to get people all over the United States to know who he was. His well-organized, down-home campaign worked. Jimmy got lots of attention and convinced people he would bring honesty to the government. In 1976, Democratic candidate Jimmy Carter just barely beat Republican President Jerry Ford.

President Jimmy Carter and First Lady Rosalynn Carter walk from the Capitol to the White House during the president's inauguration parade. Carter was the first president to walk rather than ride to the White House after his inauguration.

Jimmy Carter never had an easy time as president. He pretty much insisted on doing things his way. Members of Congress were used to having more involvement in important decisions. Soon, they became annoyed with the new president.

Jimmy Carter insisted on acting more like an ordinary, everyday person than a U.S. president. He wore inexpensive suits and sweaters. He didn't like riding in limos. He always carried his own luggage, and made sure his daughter, Amy, went to a local public school. Some people didn't like his style. They thought a president should act more important and be treated specially.

Unfortunately for President Carter, there was a worldwide energy crisis during his term. The price of oil and gas shot way up. Jimmy Carter believed the United States depended too much on getting oil from Middle Eastern countries. These countries controlled prices and could make them as high as they wanted.

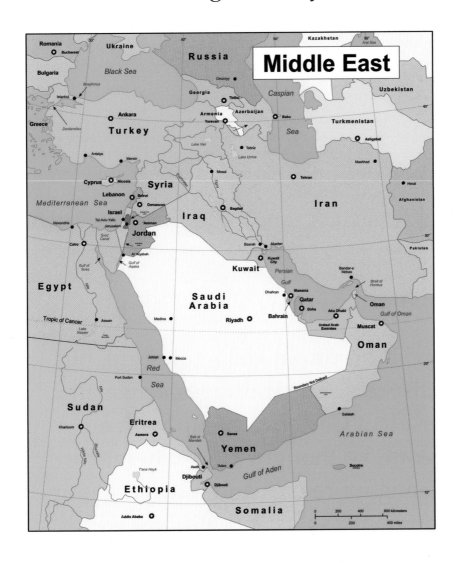

A Map of the Middle East

Americans were faced with gas shortages during Jimmy Carter's presidency.

Not only did oil prices keep going up, but there were also gasoline shortages across the country. President Carter came up with an energy program he thought would help. He suggested using more coal and natural gas and experimenting with solar and wind power.

President Carter thought individuals and businesses should be more responsible and stop wasting energy. Even though he was right, some people thought President Carter was scolding them. This didn't help his popularity at all. When it came to human rights, Jimmy Carter was never afraid to criticize the governments of countries who treated their citizens unfairly. This irritated some world leaders, especially those in the Soviet Union. They felt President Carter was getting into areas that were none of his business.

President Carter did everything he could to make sure there was peace in the world. One of his biggest successes was getting the leaders of Israel and Egypt to agree on a peace plan. These two countries were bitter enemies. Now, thanks to President Carter, there was a chance for them to live together in peace.

President Carter played an important role in helping Egyptian President Anwar Sadat (left) and Israeli Prime Minister Menachem Begin (right) reach an agreement during the 1978 peace talks at Camp David in Maryland.

Militant Iranian students display an American hostage to the crowd outside the U.S. Embassy in Tehran, Iran, in November 1979.

In 1979, an event took place that would become President Carter's biggest problem. During a revolution in the Middle East, anti-American Iranians took more than sixty U.S. citizens from the American embassy and held them hostage. Most of the Americans were held captive for over a year. As hard as he tried to get the hostages released, there was little President Carter was able to do.

Each year, Jimmy and Rosalynn Carter spend a week working with Habitat for Humanity, an organization that builds decent housing for people in need.

Jimmy Carter eventually worked out a deal to release the hostages. It wasn't in time to help him win the 1980 election, though. By then, many voters felt President Carter was a poor leader. Jimmy Carter was very disappointed. He knew he had done his best.

Even if he wasn't considered a great president, Jimmy Carter became an excellent former president. He has dedicated his life working for world peace, making sure human rights everywhere are respected, and helping poor and needy people. In 2002, Jimmy Carter was even awarded the Nobel Peace Prize, one of the world's most respected honors.